Nathaniel Appleton

A Faithful and Wise Servant

had in honour, throughout the churches - A discourse occasioned by the

much lamented death of the Rev. Edward Wigglesworth, D.D. Hollis

professor of divinity in Harvard College, Cambridge

Nathaniel Appleton

A Faithful and Wise Servant
*had in honour, throughout the churches - A discourse occasioned by the much
lamented death of the Rev. Edward Wigglesworth, D.D. Hollis professor of divinity
in Harvard College, Cambridge*

ISBN/EAN: 9783337196363

Printed in Europe, USA, Canada, Australia, Japan

Cover: Foto ©Andreas Hilbeck / pixelio.de

More available books at **www.hansebooks.com**

Mr. *Appleton*'s

DISCOURSE

Occasioned by the DEATH of

Dr. *Wigglesworth*

A faithful and wife Servant, had in Honour, throughout the Churches.

A

DISCOURSE

Occafioned by the much lamented DEATH

OF THE

Rev. EDWARD WIGGLESWORTH, D.D.

HOLLIS Profeffor of Divinity in HARVARD College, Cambridge;

Who departed this Life, January 16. 1765. In the 73d Year of his Age.

Having faithfully and laudably difcharged the Office of PROFESSOR, for more than 42 Years.

By *NATHANIEL APPLETON*, A.M.
Paftor of the firft Church in CAMBRIDGE.

Forafmuch as an excellent fpirit, and knowledge, and underftanding,——and fhewing of hard fentences, and diffolving of doubts, were found in the fame Daniel. ——And they that be wife fhall fhine as the brightnefs of the firmament. The Prophet DANIEL.

BOSTON, NEW-ENGLAND:
Printed by RICHARD and SAMUEL DRAPER, and THOMAS and JOHN FLEET, 1765.

A

Funeral Sermon

ON THE

Rev. Dr. WIGGLESWORTH.

❦❦❦❦❦❦❦❦❦❦❦❦❦

2 CORINTHIANS, VIII. 18.

——The Brother, whose Praise is in the Gospel, throughout all the Churches.

AS we are not told who this brother was that the apostle sent with Titus on a special occasion to Corinth; so there can be only conjecture about the matter. Several names are mentioned, such as *Barnabas*, that son of consolation, and *Silas*, and *Apollos*, and *Mark*; and especially *Luke*, who wrote the gospel which goes by his name, upon the account of which gospel he became famous in all the churches. The extraordinary character here given of this brother might be as descriptive of him, and as clearly point him out at that day, as if he had been expressly mentioned

by

by name. But it is not material, nor to our prefent purpofe, to know who he was : For all that we have to do is with the fhort, but high commendation which is given of him.

AND here we may obferve firft of all that he is ftiled *a brother;* by which is underftood not merely a chriftian brother, a believer, and brother in Chrift : But a brother and companion in the gofpel miniftry; a *fellow worker unto the kingdom of God* : Equally engaged and concerned with the other minifters, in eftablifhing and promoting the gofpel.

IN the next place, we may obferve the commendation that is given of this brother minifter.—— He was *had in praife* and high commendation.—— There were excellent accomplifhments, and amiable qualities in him, which fhone forth fo confpicuoufly, that he was highly efteemed and greatly refpected. We may fuppofe he was in high reputation for his eminent gifts of knowledge, wifdom, faith, zeal, and ftedfaftnefs, with which he was endowed by the fpirit of God.

FURTHER, let us confider the *extenfivenefs* of this high efteem and reputation he was in.—Whofe praife is throughout *all the churches.* Which is to be underftood not only of the members ; but of the minifters of the churches. His gifts and accomplifhments were fo fuperiour and extenfive, that they were not confined to any particular church, or to any private and retired corner of the vineyard, where

where his gifts and graces would be out of general
view, and very much buried in obfcurity : But God
fo ordered it that his rare accomplifhments fhould
be publickly known and acknowledged. "We may
fuppofe his preaching, his writings, and other mi-
nifterial fervices, rendered him very famous even
in all the churches.. Very likely he was well
known to the apoftles, and other minifters of Chrift
in general, who difcerned the excellent qualities
he was endowed with ; and gave forth fuch high
commendations of him, as fpread his fame through
all the churches ; fo that they were all filled with
the high praifes of him.

AGAIN, let us confider the particular point for
which he was more efpecially had in fuch high
reputation : And that was with reference to the
gofpel. Whofe praife is in the GOSPEL'; or for the
gofpel. Whatever his knowledge and accomplifhments were as to other things ; yet it was for his
knowledge of Chrift, and of the great things of the
gofpel, that he became fo famous in the churches.
He was well inftructed, and, we may fuppofe,
eminent for his knowledge, in the things of God
and the diftinguifhing points of chriftianity. And
if this brother was *Luke* the evangelift (which was
the prevailing opinion of the ancients) he was eminently inftructed in the gofpel hiftory ; and fo in
the doctrines and principles of chriftianity. We may
well fuppofe him to be mighty in the fcriptures,
and that he, like the great apoftle Paul, *reafoned*
with the people out of the holy fcriptures, opening
and

and alleging that Jefus was the Chrift. Acts xvii. 2, 3. His difcourfes on thofe points were highly efteemed; and great weight was laid on his judgment in difficult points of the gofpel, in matters of controverfy, or of doubtful difputation.

But then we may conclude further, that his praife in the gofpel, throughout all the churches, was for the known ftedfaftnefs of his faith, and the uniformity of his temper and behaviour with this gofpel he profeffed, preached up, and recommended to others. His knowledge and faith, his temper and manner of life, were all of a piece, and according to the gofpel: Without which we cannot fuppofe that his praife would have been in all the churches.

Lastly, I would obferve the emphatic article that is here affixed to this brother. *The* brother. It is not faid we have fent with Titus *a* brother, but *the* brother, by way of diftinction, and eminency above the other brethren in the miniftry: And as one peculiarly fitted for the fervice upon which he was fent. He was pitched upon as *the* brother, the very man above all the reft to be employed in the fervice he was fent upon. No man like minded, no man fo eminently fitted for the bufinefs he was employed in.

After fuch a large opening the text (by which the fuitablenefs thereof to the prefent difpenfation of Divine Providence may very obvioufly appear to every one) I proceed for the further illuftration of the fubject to confider, 1ft,

1ft, *Some of thofe gofpel qualifications which de- fervedly intitle a man to univerfal praife ; to the praife of all the churches.*

2dly, *To fet forth what a diftinguifhing favour and bleffed attainment it is, to be juftly intitled to univerfal praife.*

3dly, *Make fome proper improvement, fuited to the folemn and forrowful o⬤⬤on that leads us to thefe meditations.* ⬤

I. LET us confider fome of *thofe gofpel qua- lifications, which defervedly intitle a man to uni- verfal praife ; the praife of all the churches.*

AND here I will begin with

1ft. *Extenfive knowledge in the great things of the gofpel.*

KNOWLEDGE is an effential article in a great and good man. *For the foul to be without knowledge, it is not good.* * And there is no knowledge fo fublime, fo enlarging, and enobling to the foul, as the knowledge of God, and the things of God; the knowledge of Chrift, and the way to falvation by him : *And this is life eternal, to know thee the only true God, and Jefus Chrift whom thou haft fent.*† The learned and great apoftle Paul, who muft be allowed to be a good judge of knowledge and

B   . learning,

* Prov. XIX. 2.   † John XVII. 3.

learning, as to the excellency and ufefulnefs of it, declares that he counted all things but lofs, for the excellency of the knowledge of Chrift Jefus his Lord.* In the chriftian fcheme of falvation, which is contained in the holy fcriptures, are hid all the treafures of divine wifdom and knowledge; confequently it muft needs be a very laudable attainment, to have a good and thorough acquaintance with the holy fcriptures, thofe oracles of divine truth : To be able not only ⬛cite the words of the holy fcriptures; but to fee and underftand the meaning of the fame. It is very praife-worthy to be able fo to fearch the fcriptures, as to compare tranfla-tions with the original; and to compare fpiritual things with fpiritual; one portion of fcripture with another; fo as, inftead of being carried away with the found of words, to gain the true fenfe and meaning of the feveral places; and thereby to gain a clear and comprehenfive view of the gofpel fcheme of falvation; and fo of the various truths and duties therein contained.

Moreover, this knowledge of the gofpel that is truly laudable, and would recommend to public efteem, is a good acquaintance with the various fenfes that have been put upon places of holy fcripture; and fo the various fentiments, fyftems and principles of chriftianity, that have or do prevail in the world, whereby they may be able to put a mark upon dangerous errors, which have been broach-ed by ignorant men, who have wrefted the holy fcriptures; and to point out the truth as it is in Jefus.

FURTHERMORE,

* Phil. III. 8.

. FURTHERMORE, another very laudable point of knowledge in the things of God, is to underſtand the ground and foundation of our hóly religion; and to get acquainted ſo far both with the internal and external evidence of the divine authority of the holy ſcriptures, and ſo of the truth of chriſtianity, as to be able to convince gainſayers, and to vindicate the glorious truths of the goſpel from the captious cavils, or mere ſubtle objections ſtarted by *men of corrupt minds, given to perverſe diſputings, and deſtitute of the truth :* And to be able to ſet in a ſtrong and convincing light, the arguments to prove the holy ſcriptures to be given by inſpiration of God; and conſequently that the goſpel ſcheme of ſalvation is built upon a ſure foundation, upon which we may ſafely venture our ſouls and the eternal concerns of them.

Now, ſuch an extenſive knowledge of the goſpel, and ſo of the foundations of our holy religion, is ſuch a neceſſary and excellent attainment, that thoſe who make a laudable proficiency herein, merit highly of the church of God. Such men have been in one age and another the pillars of the church; the external props by which the church has been kept from ſinking into utter ignorance and infidelity.

2dly. Soundneſs of principles ; adhering cloſely to the goſpel, without adding thereto, or diminiſhing, or varying therefrom, is very praiſe-worthy.

B 2   FOR,

For, altho' orthodoxy, or foundnefs of principles, may be an uncertain phrafe, inafmuch as the various fects that are in the world, lay claim to this character; yet, as chriftians of all denominations profefs the gofpel to be the only fure and unerring rule of faith and manners; fo thofe principles muft be foundeft, which come the neareft to the ftandard. Confequently, thofe perfons who not only profeffedly, but really endeavour to fquare their faith and practice by the doctrines and precepts of the gofpel, are to be had in honour. And where this evidently appears to be the care and endeavour of any perfons, fo as neither to preach, publifh or vent any thing as a neceffary article of faith, but what is plainly demonftrated by the word of God; it muft needs recommend them to the church of God, which is built upon the foundation of the apoftles and prophets, Jefus Chrift being the chief corner ftone.* And therefore thofe teachers who have fo much knowledge, wifdom and humility, as not to be wife above what is written, and make this their conftant inquiry, in all their fearches after divine truths, *what faith the fcripture?* and whenever they fpeak in a way of teaching, fpeak as the oracles of God; and appeal to thofe written facred oracles, according to the true genuine meaning of the fame, for the truth of what they affert, are highly to be commended, and deferve the praifes of all the churches of Chrift: Which will appear by confidering the dreadful errors, fuperftitions, corruptions, and idolatries, the church fell into, when they departed from this

only

* Eph. II. 20.

only unerring rule, and fet up an infallible head on earth; and taught for doctrines the traditions and commandments of men.

AND how well did thofe glorious worthies deferve of the church of Chrift, who boldly and courageoufly began a reformation, and ftrenuoufly endeavoured to reduce the church to its original foundation, the holy fcriptures? And how juftly are the names of thofe firft reformers handed down with honour throughout all the proteftant churches in the world? But, inafmuch as even the reformed churches have not gotten fo compleatly upon the original bafis as is to be defired; it muft needs be very praife-worthy for thofe who are fet up to be teachers of others, to labour to fix them more and more upon the gofpel foundation, without the particular fchemes, fyftems, or inventions of men; or indeed fo much as the expreffions of men in fuch grand myfterious points, wherein *we know not how to order our fpeech by reafon of darknefs.*

3dly. *The gift of opening the holy fcriptures; fetting forth the truths and duties contained therein, in a true, diftinct and clear light,* is what recommends teachers to the churches of the Lord Jefus.

THIS implies a capacious mind, a clear head, extenfive knowledge, diftinct ideas, and reach of thought, obtained, or improved, by much reading and ftudy, a careful weighing matters, and laying them together. And furely fuch natural endowments,

ments, improved by·clofe application to meditation
and reading, juftly claim the high efteem of the
churches of Chrift. And fuch will be refpected
and honoured by all the lovers of truth, and the
diligent fincere inquirers after it. How are perfons
inftructed, and greatly edified, who fet at the feet
of fuch learned doctors whofe ideas lie clear and diftinct ; and what benefit have the written labours of
fuch men been to the chriftian world ? And how
have their learned expofitions, wherein they have
unfolded the holy fcriptures, and their other inge-
nious and judicious difcourfes, brought and preferved
light and knowledge in the church ? And how have
the names and memories of fuch learned authors
been handed down and fpread abroad in the chriftian church, with high honour and efteem ?

4thly. THE gift of confirming divine truths and
enforcing duties, in a ftrong, convincing and
moving·manner, juftly claims the praifes of all
chriftians.

THIS is a gift as ufeful and neceffary, in its place,
as the former, for the church of Chrift. It is not
fufficient to fet. truths and duties before perfons,
merely to enlighten their underftandings, and enlarge their minds ; but, as all divine truths have
reference to practice, to which there is a natural
backwardnefs, and great oppofition, from the world,
the things of the world, the corrupt cuftoms of the
world, the enticements and the examples of finners ;

fo

fo there needs warm addreffes to the confcience, to the paffions and affections of the foul, yea to all the fprings of action. People need, not only to be told their duty, and fhown what it is; but to be urged to it, and in a moving manner be expoftulated with about it. Confequently, the compleat preacher, or teacher, will have his eafy, clear and plain inftructions warm'd and animated, as if his tongue had been juft touched with *a live coal from off the altar.* His writings will be pungent, as well as clear and pertinent; and all the great arguments of the gofpel for a chriftian temper and practice, will be fet in fuch array, as may ferve not only to excite and engage the attention, but to roufe the confcience, to enkindle the affections; yea, and with the concurring influence of the divine fpirit, to perfuade the will, and convert the man. And Oh! how much is the church of God obliged to fuch awakening preachers; and for fuch practical and pathetic writings of theirs which are extant, and lodged in chriftian families! And what a multitude of precious faints will rife up at the judgment and call fuch preachers and authors bleffed, for the bleffed effects of their faithful labours upon their fouls? And with what refpect and affection are fuch faithful fervants of Chrift fpoken of among the people of God, and how are their practical writings recommended, fpread, and handed down from one generation to another?

5thly. A fpecial gift of *difcerning of fpirits;* accurately diftinguifhing between *truth* and *error;*

error ; between *greater* and *leſſer* matters of chriſtianity ; between things *clear* and *plain,* and thoſe that are *doubtful ;* between *eſſentials* and *circumſtantials* in religion.

THIS is a moſt uſeful and even neceſſary gift for preachers and teachers of the goſpel ; and the want of it has cauſed the greateſt diſturbances and confuſions in the church. Truth and error, altho' eſſentially different from each other, yet oftentimes put on ſuch ſimilar appearances, that it requires a ſharp and penetrating eye to diſcern the difference, ſo as to diſtinguiſh the truth from the error. Error is oftentimes gilded over with ſuch ſpecious and plauſible arguments, and communicated in ſuch artful and equivocal terms, that miniſters, as well as others, have ſwallowed them down as truths ; and only ſome ſingular gift of diſcerning has been able to diſcover the error, and the danger thereof that was couched therein.

BUT then again, what ſevere conteſts have there been among the churches of Chriſt ; and how have they been thrown into feuds and quarrels? How have they loſt their charity one for another? How have they ſeparated and withdrawn communion from each other? Yea, how have they in their turns perſecuted one another even unto death? And all this for want of diſcerning between the greater and the leſſer matters of the goſpel, the eſſentials and only circumſtantials of religion ! But now, when God endows any of his ſervants with

an

an eminent fpirit of difcerning in thefe matters, fo as to fee what *faith* that is which was once delivered to the faints, to be contended for; and what are matters of lefs importance, and not worth contending about; what matter is this of thankfgiving to God? and how highly do fuch deferve of all the churches, who give them to fee that the matters in which they differ are not worth ftriving or breaking charity about; and who are inftrumental of perfuading chriftians, notwithftanding the little differences in opinion and practice, to maintain charity and communion one with another? How defervedly are they in the praife of all the churches within their knowledge and influence, who are able in any meafure, with the wifdom and difcerning of the apoftle Paul, to conciliate them in matters of difference about leffer things, as he did, Rom. xiv. about eating, or not eating certain meats, or obferving, and not obferving certain days; concerning which he advifes not to judge nor to defpife one another; but, being fully perfuaded in their own minds, he would have them charitably to believe as to each other, that they did what they thought moft pleafing to Chrift. *He that eateth, eateth to the Lord; for he giveth God thanks : He that eateth not, to the Lord he eateth not, and giveth God thanks.*

6thly, *Zeal for the great truths and duties of chriftianity ; but duly tempered with charity and prudence, challenges high honour and refpect from the churches of Chrift.*

C

ALTHOUGH

ALTHOUGH there is a blind furious zeal about matters comparatively fmall, which is to be dreaded; yet there is a zeal that is truly laudable. *It is good to be zealoufly affected always in a good thing.** And Chrift purifies to himfelf a peculiar people, *zealous of good works.*† How commendable muft it be for teachers and preachers, who are fet for the defence of the gofpel, to appear zealous, bold and courageous for the truth, fo as to defend it againft all the daring attempts of deifts and infidels, and fuch like vile oppofers of chriftianity? Surely the church of God is greatly indebted to thofe chriftian heroes, who inftead of being afhamed of the gofpel of Chrift, or afraid to appear in his caufe, have openly profeffed him before perfecuting kings and emperors, and have facrificed their very lives in the caufe; and fubmitted to the moft cruel tortures that men or devils could invent, rather than re-nounce the chriftian caufe? Thefe glorious mar-tyrs are defervedly had in praife throughout all the churches; and their names had in everlafting re-membrance, whofe zeal and courage conquered the heathen rage, and caufed the gofpel fo to fpread, that it became a general obfervation that *the blood of the martyrs was the feed of the church.*

AND as to thofe who have not been called to refift unto blood; but yet have had a zeal to appear openly in the defence of chriftianity, and of any of its important truths and duties, they deferve very highly of the church: For if it had not been for fuch

zealous

* Gal. IV. 18.   † Tit. II. 14.

zealous and careful watchmen upon the walls, to give
faithful and feafonable warning, the church would
have been robbed of one important truth and duty
of chriftianity after another, till it would have been
ftript of every thing that is purely chriftian, and
carried back to the religion. of the heathen, or
fomething worfe.

BUT then, a zeal that is truly commendable
will not be fevere and cruel, though it fhould have
power in its hand ; but is regulated by charity and
goodnefs. It is not a zeal that rafhly thinketh or
fpeaketh evil of others; but being qualified with
love and charity, don't allow itfelf to think any
evil, without fufficient foundation for it; but hopeth
all things, and believeth all things it poffibly can,
upon any good foundation, in favour of them;
ready to put as favourable conftructions upon their
fentiments and ways as they will poffibly bear:
This zeal is alfo directed by wifdom and prudence, carefully avoiding all rafhnefs and precipi-
tancy, and every thing that is fierce and cruel,
which fiery zeal prompts to ; but wifely confiders
the perfons with whom it has to do, and the times and
circumftances of things.——And now how much are
the churches indebted to fuch who though zealous
for God and his caufe, are candid and charitable,
prudent and cautious in all their meafures ? And
how are uproars in towns and churches ftilled,
party rage and fury allayed, and all things brought
to peace and kept in it, by the happy influence of
fuch a temper ?

C 2

7thly. *Stedfaſtneſs in the truths and ways of God is highly commendable.*

By which I mean not a rigid fixedneſs or inflexibility againſt arguments ſufficient to change our minds; for this would be obſtinacy and perverſneſs, rather than a rational or gracious ſtedfaſtneſs; which ſtedfaſtneſs is oppoſite to that fickleneſs of temper, and wavering diſpoſition, that keeps men ſo looſe and unhinged, that they hardly know their own minds, much leſs may others depend upon them.

Now ſuch unſtable ſouls, liable as the weathercock to be turned by the wind, and ſo to be like children toſſed to and fro by every wind of doctrine, very much diſparage their character. *Unſtable as water, they ſhall not excell.**

Whereas the ſtedfaſt man is he, who having examined the ground of his faith and practice, and finding himſelf upon a good foundation, remains fixed and ſteady. He is not ſuddenly moved by ſophiſtical and ſubtle arguments, or plauſible appearances of things; but will examine and obſerve things carefully; and not change his mind or conduct, till upon a careful and thorough weighing of the matter, he finds it reaſonable.

And ſurely it muſt be highly to the commendation of ſuch as are appointed the guides and inſtructors of others, that they be firm and ſteady in their principles, and able to defend them. And theſe

† Gen. XLV. 4.

thefe churches are greatly indebted to fuch fteady and faithful guides, to whom, under God, it is very much owing that they have hitherto been preferved upon their foundation; when they have been fo vehemently affaulted by ignorant and illiterate intruders, who have thrown many of the churches into confufion, and threatned their over-throw. If it had not been for a number of fteady chriftians, minifters and fpiritual guides (of whom the late deceafed among us was an eminent one) thefe churches would have been much fhaken, if not overthrown; therefore fuch juftly claim a praife thro' all the churches.

8thly. *I may add that diligence, conftancy and acti-vity are very recommending qualities.*

These added to the forementioned qualities, render a man very illuftrious, and fpread his name and fame throughout the churches, far and near. It was by the diligence, the activity, and the abun-dant labours of fome upon facred, and others upon ecclefiaftical record, that they have rendered them-felves famous in all ages of the church, even to this day.——But I may not enlarge. Therefore,

9thly. *Sincerely aiming to honour God with all his gifts, and carefully endeavouring to exemplify all the graces and virtues of the chriftian in his own life, muft needs recommend to the praife of all the churches who fhall fee and hear of the fame.*

THIS

THIS is the crowning point of any great man's character. It is THIS that makes the man's face to ſhine. It is THIS that puts a luſtre upon all the rich endowments of nature, or of education. It is THIS that adorns the man in every office, in every ſtation and relation of life. It is THIS that puts a gloſs, yea a real beauty and excellency upon all performances. Then it is that miniſters and other doctors of divinity recommend their diſcourſes, and ſet forth the beauty and excellency of divine truths, and give a certain force and energy to them, viz. when they exemplify their doctrines and their counſels in their own temper and carriage. When miniſters and ſpiritual guides live as the goſpel teaches them, and as they teach others from the goſpel, even *ſoberly*, and *righteouſly*, and *godly*, in the world: Then, I ſay, they do in an eminent manner adorn the doctrine of God our Saviour. THIS *will cauſe their lights to ſhine before men; and others ſeeing and hearing of their good works;* of their exemplary piety, holineſs and goodneſs, will not only have them in great reputation and honour, but will be induced to be followers of them; and from their bright example to glorify our Father which is in heaven.

II. LET us now proceed to conſider what a *diſtinguiſhing favour and bleſſed attainment it is, to have ſuch endowments, natural or acquired, and ſuch a gracious temper and behaviour, as juſtly to claim the praiſes of all the churches.*

It

IT is an high commendation which is here given of this brother minifter in the text, *That his praife in the gofpel was throughout all the churches,* intimating hereby that there was fomething uncommon in him; and that God had enabled him, in a very diftinguifhing manner, to recommend himfelf to the high efteem and praife of all the churches; which fuppofes the forementioned, and fuch like accomplifhments, in an eminent degree, were found in him. *His praife in all the churches,* is not to be underftood as if he was only a very popular man, who by voice and gefture, and flow of words, gained the vulgar popular applaufe; but that he had fuch real excellencies and accomplifhments as recommended him to the apoftles and minifters, and to all the wife and underftanding and judicious among them; who were able to difcern the things that differ.

AND that it is a diftinguifhing favour and bleffed attainment to have fuch endowments of mind, and fuch other good qualities, as juftly recommend to the high efteem of all wife and good men, will appear, if we briefly confider a few things.

1ft. *That they are only great and good qualities which will recommend to the efteem and refpect of wife, great and good men.*

THE illiterate vulgar and weak people may be carried away with noife and fhow, and fome little popular arts, without any thing fubftantially good and excellent. The brother in our text was
not

not fuch an one : But his qualifications were fuch
as recommended him to the wife and the beft
judges of true worth : Confequently, there muft
have been excellent endowments and fuperiour
qualities found in him, to recommend to univerfal
efteem.——And now it muft needs be a great
favour and fpecial bleffing, to be fo richly endowed
as to gain, and that very defervedly, an univerfal
efteem. Every good gift, and every perfect gift,
is from above, and cometh down from the Father
of lights. He is the former of our bodies, and the
Father of our fpirits; and he forms and unites
them together in a manner we know not how;
from whence arife the various capacities, geniufes
and inclinations among the children of men. And
he who has the difpofing of all things in providence,
orders out the various advantages, and gives the
various inclinations to improve the fame, for the
enlarging the mind, and enriching it with a greater
variety of ufeful knowledge. And whenever their
natural powers and acquired knowledge are fanctified, and converted to the greateft and beft pur-
pofes, it is by the grace of God. And therefore
when there are fuch diftinguifhing endowments of
nature, providence, and grace, found in any, as
give them a diftinguifhing efteem among the wife
and good, it muft be looked upon as a diftinguifhing favour to fuch, and fhould be acknowledged by
them and their friends to the glory of God. For
what have any which may claim diftinguifhing efteem,
but what they have received? and therefore, whilft
fuch receive honour and praife of men, they fhould
give the glory to God.   2dly.

2dly. *It is a rare thing to have these good qualities
so united in the same subject, and in so conspicuous a manner as to gain universal esteem and
reputation.*

Those good qualities which deserve commendation and praise, are for the most part dispersed
among the children of men. To this man is given
one eminent gift, to that man is given another. Some
have superiour natural powers; but no education to
cultivate and enlarge them. Others have good natural powers, and good education; but they have
violent passions, suddenly moved and carried to great
excess; besides other bad natural tempers. Others
again have all these advantages, good capacities,
good temper, good education to the great enlargement of their minds; but no grace to sanctify
them, and fit them for their master's use; and
so they cannot be in that high esteem in the
churches, and with the faithful in Christ Jesus.
But then again, supposing the man excellent for natural powers and for great improvement of his mind
by education, and a good natural temper, and all
sanctified by divine grace; yet, alas! how often has
the character of such an one been slurred by some
sin or folly that he has fallen into? which has been
as *the dead fly in the ointment of the apothecary,
that sendeth forth a stinking savour,* and brings a
blot and disgrace *upon him that is in reputation for
wisdom and honour.**

Lastly here, There are some excellent persons
who upon all accounts deserve and have the high

commendations

* Eccles. X. 1.

commendations of all who are acquainted with them: But they are not much known; their light is as it were put under a bufhel; their lot is in fome remote and retired corner of the vineyard; and fo they live and die pretty much in obfcurity. So that, upon the whole, to have perfons of fuch fuperiour accomplifhments, fanctified and adorned by divine grace, free from any blot or blemifh in their character, and thefe placed as a city fet upon a hill, to be feen and known of all men, is a very rare thing, and confequently to be taken notice of and acknowledged as a diftinguifhing favour and blefling.

3dly. *It is a fpecial favour, as it gives to fuch great advantages for being eminently ufeful in the world.*

REPUTATION and efteem give a man great advantage for doing good; and the higher and more extenfive his character rifes, fo much the greater opportunity it gives him of being ufeful to mankind. The fentiments of fuch a man will be much regarded; his judgment will be highly efteemed; his counfel will be fought after and hearkened unto; his advice on particular points of difficulty will come with weight; and his example will be very influential; and being gracioufly inclined to do all the good he can, it is not eafy to think how extenfively ufeful fuch a man is to the family, to the town, and to every fociety with which he is connected; yea, and to the church of God in general.——And now the more ufeful God

makes

makes us in the world, fo much the more favour he
fhows to us, and fo much the more honour he
confers upon us.

4thly. *As the man highly and defervedly efteemed*
implies the faithful and the wife fervant ; fo he
will receive the diftinguifhing rewards of fuch.

WE are fpeaking of men who are defervedly
efteemed and honoured as the faithful fervants of
Chrift; and as fuch they will be not only efteemed
and praifed through the churches of Chrift, but
they fhall have the high approbation of their judge;
and from high efteem among the faints on earth,
fhall be received to glory, honour and immortality
in heaven; and by how much they have diftinguifhed themfelves, according to their abilities and
opportunities, in the fervice of God, for the honour
of Chrift and the good of men, fo much the
greater will be their reward in heaven; and fo
much more open and abundant entrance fhall be
miniftred to them into the everlafting kingdom. All
which ferves to fhow what a fpecial favour it is to
have fuperiour abilities, fo fanctified and faithfully
improved, as fhall be not only with reputation and
honour in the church of God; but with the approbation of our judge. For this is the way to have that
blefled *euge* full of honour, comfort and happinefs
pronounced upon us : *Well done good and faithful*
fervant——enter into the joy of thy Lord.*

D 2   LET

* Matt. XXV. 21.

LET us now proceed to make fome *improvement* and *application* of thefe meditations.

1ft. WE learn from what has been faid that *God is thankfully to be acknowledged by all whom he largely endows with fuch gifts and graces, as defervedly give them great efteem and an high character in the church of God.*

THE gifts of nature, even all the powers of the mind, with the natural genius, difpofition and temper; and all the advantages for improvement and enlargement; and all that virtuous and gracious turn of mind, with good behaviour; and all the laudable actions and performances, whereby perfons recommend themfelves to the high efteem of others, are from God even from the very firft to the laft: And that very honour and efteem that arifes from hence comes of him; and is a favour of divine providence thankfully to be acknowledged to God's glory, and improved to his honour.

GOD's giving a man high efteem and reputation, gives him great advantages of doing much for the honour of God and the good of mankind: And in this way he is to exprefs his thankfulnefs to God for any fuch diftinguifhing favour. The fentiments, the principles, the counfels, the admonitions, the examples of fuch will be weighty and influential, in proportion to the character they bear, and the efteem and honour they are had in, among mankind. Surely then it concerns fuch to fhow their thankfulnefs

fulnefs to God for his diftinguifhing favours to
them; by being fo much the more careful in all
their fayings, and in all their writings they fend
forth into the world : And fo much the more circumfpect in all their conduct, becaufe the eyes
of people naturally fix upon them: Nothing is
more common than for perfons to defend themfelves
in that which is ill, and unguarded, and fo cannot
otherwife be excufed; by faying it is no more
than fuch and fuch who bear the beft of characters
have faid or done. Confequently fuch men whom
God favours with high reputation and character,
cannot better fhow their gratitude to him for the
fame, than by a moft guarded, circumfpect, exemplary converfation, diligently employing their gifts,
and improving their intereft in men's hearts for the
honour of God, the increafe of religion, and fo
the beft good of mankind.

2dly. THE fubject before us teaches us *That it is
    but a laudable ambition, to endeavour juftly to
    deferve a univerfal good character.*

THE apoftle fpeaks of it as a high commendation of the brother in our text, *that he was had in
praife throughout all the churches,* and confequently
it was to his honour, that he laboured fo to acquit
himfelf as to merit fuch univerfal praife.

THE love of fame or praife is a natural paffion
formed in man to ferve fome great and good pur-
pofes, and to prompt men to labour to excell in
                                        things

things great and good : And this paffion under due regulation ferves as a noble and powerful fpur to great and good, but difficult and dangerous enter-prizes. But this as well as the other ufeful paffions of the foul is degenerated and corrupted ; and fo is apt to run into extremes.

WITH fome this laudable ambition degenerates into *fordid meannefs, and a criminal difregard of charaĉler ;* they are carelefs what men fay or think of them ; and are fo negligent of the good opinion of others, that they will do nothing to deferve their good efteem ; and fet fo light by a good name (though it be better than great riches) that they will facrifice it, and expofe themfelves to the con-tempt of all wife and good men, for the fake of gratifying fome filthy and brutifh luft.

THE other extreme is, when this laudable am-bition degenerates into *pride :* Some men are more concerned to have praife and honour than to deferve it ; and indulge fuch an exceffive love of fame as, to take unjuftifiable methods for the gaining it. Inftead of obferving the wife man's rule,* *Let ano-ther man praife thee, and not thine own mouth ; a ftranger, and not thine own lips,* they will praife themfelves ; and will do every thing in an oftenta-tious vain-glorious manner, that they may have praife and glory of men ; to the neglect of fuch duties and fervices as are out of the fight of men ; they aim only at the appearance and not the reality of good-nefs ; and will vilify others to exalt themfelves, and fecretly wound other mens charaĉters to ad-vance their own.

BUT

* Prov. XXVII. 2.

But now happy is the man, who has wisdom
and grace to steer between these two extremes;
who has a due regard to character, but endeavours
to deserve it, as well as have it; who desires
and seeks no further praise or commendation than
he has just claim to; and who endeavours to acquit
himself faithfully in every office and relation of
life he sustains, and leaves it with God to give or
with-hold the praise.

3dly. *What a great blessing to a people, thankfully
to be acknowledged, when God raises up persons,
and qualifies them after such a manner as to
deserve the praises and high commendations of all
the churches; even of all wise, serious and
good men.*

THESE are indeed the *excellent ones in the earth.*
They are the *salt of the earth.* These are *the
light of the world.* They are *the pillars of the
churches, and the glory of Christ;* and the means of
preserving the churches from sinking into ignorance
and degenerating into corruption. It is by such
men's being raised up in one age of the church,
and another, that the truths and principles of
christianity, according to the scriptures, have been
preserved, and even rescued and separated from the
dregs of ignorance and corruption, which the
church in some former ages was sunk into; and
the truth as it is in Jesus, and in his gospel, made
to shine forth, with such a degree of clearness as
now

now it does. Surely the churches of God are greatly indebted to fuch able and faithful men. But O! what obligations are chriftians under to God, and to the Lord Jefus Chrift, who has, from time to time, raifed up fuch men, and enriched them with fuch excellent gifts! Surely it becomes chriftians to be thankful for the gifts beftowed upon others, as well as upon themfelves: For fuperiour gifts beftowed upon any perfons are for the public good; and therefore we fhould all rejoice in them, and be thankful for them.

4thly. Consequently, *the death and departure of perfons of diftinguifhing worth and character ought to be taken notice of as a public lofs, and the hearts of people duely affected therewith.*

As for thofe whofe praife is in all the churches, when God takes them away by death, it becomes churches to be humble under his holy hand; and I believe you will every one agree that God is calling us at this time to take a folemn and humble notice of fuch a difpenfation of his holy providence the laft week, in the death and departure of the *Rev. Dr.* Wigglesworth, *Hollis Profeffor of Divinity in the College,* whofe remains were interred the laft evening. The juft claim he had to the high commendation and character in my text, led me to the fubject; he being a reverend brother, whofe praife in the gofpel is defervedly had throughout the churches; yea, we may apply
the

the character of *Demetrius* unto him, of whom it
is faid, *That he hath good report of all men, and
of the truth itfelf.* *

THE great former of all things, who defigned
him for a very important ftation of life, relating
to his gofpel kingdom, formed him originally with
many very fuperiour powers of the mind, diftin-
guifhingly fitted for fuch a fervice. Altho' God
gave him but a flender conftitution of body, yet he
was very liberal to him in the various faculties of
his foul, which perhaps were promoted and brought
forth to greater advantage by the tendernefs and
delicacy of his bodily frame. So that in his very
make and conftitution there was fuch an extenfivenefs and reach of thought, fuch a quicknefs and
clearnefs of apprehenfion, fuch a foundnefs of judgment, fuch an acutenefs and ftrength of reafoning,
fuch accuracy of expreffion; and all thefe accompa-
nied with fuch a calm, fedate and difpaffionate temper
as are rarely to be met with in the fame fubject.

HAVING had the advantage of a liberal education, he enlarged and ftored his mind with treafures of ufeful knowledge. And as he purpofed,
by the will of God, to employ his life in the
gofpel miniftry, fo divinity, and the things of the
gofpel, and thofe which would ferve to illuftrate
and confirm the fame, were the fubjects that he
chiefly employed his mind in the ftudy of. And
altho' he ftood candidate for the gofpel miniftry,
and went on in occafional preaching for fome years;

E   in

* III. Ep. John 12 ver.

in which he gave to all, but especially to the
more learned and judicious, very ample tokens of
his superiour abilities and thorough acquaintance
with sacred things; yet it appeared in a little time,
by the course of providence, that God had another
and very important business in reserve for him:
Namely, that instead of being confined to teach
and minister to one single congregation of common
christians, he should be an instructor of all the
young candidates for the gospel ministry, and train
them up in the great doctrines and principles of
christianity; and so form and fit them to go forth
into the several congregations of the Lord, and
preach the pure truths of the gospel to them; and
so to have it as his special business, to teach those
who were to be teachers and preachers to others.

To bring about this important event, behold! at that very time, God raised up a most
generous benefactor to the college, viz. the late
worthy Mr. Thomas Hollis, merchant, of
London; who among his many pious and charitable
benefactions to the college, founded a professorship
for divinity; making the same known to the corporation, desiring them to name some person to him
proper for that service. Accordingly, the distinguishing abilities of Mr. Wigglesworth were so
conspicuous, that he was unanimously nominated
and appointed to that office; in which he has,
thro' the great goodness of God, very laudably,
yea with distinguishing honour, officiated for more
than forty two years; and so has abundantly an-
swered the high recommendatory character given

of

of him by one of the corporation, and in their name, to his worthy patron. *

AND by fuch a faithful and acceptable difcharge of this office it is more efpecially that his praife comes to be in all the churches : For, altho' his occafional preaching and his printed works have fpread his fame; yet it was by the conftant attendance upon the duties of his office, that his praife has been diffufed thro'
E 2
thefe

* " There is but one thing more, Sir, which I have now to add, but it is a very great one ; the nomination of a per-fon to you, to be your firft profeffor. There is lately returned to, and is now refiding in the college, a very accomplifhed perfon for the office, in our joint opinion and judgment, Mr. *Edward Wigglefworth*, who in the year 1710 paffed his firft degree with us, and has ever fince diligently applied himfelf to the learned ftudies, and to the ftudy of divinity more efpecially. He is a perfon of known and exemplary virtue, piety, literature, modefty, meeknefs, and other chriftian ornaments. His public exercifes in the pulpit difcover a folid judgment, a clean ftile, a clear method, a bright and ftrong thought, and a facility or aptnefs to teach : And it now appears to us as if Providence may have referved him for fuch a fervice as this now before us ; which we apprehend may fuit him in all refpects, excepting his low opinion of himfelf; yet neither is he wanting in gravity, wifdom, and a fpirit of government and authority, which may be neceffary to command the reverence of others to him, in any office he may be called to."
Vid. Life and Character of Dr. Colman, p. 54, 55.

Befides the profefforfhip of divinity, the above named Mr. *Hollis* founded a profefforfhip of mathematicks, of natural and experimental philofophy; eftablifhed ten fcholar-fhips; furnifhed the college with a coftly and valuable apparatus; and fome or other of that worthy name and
family

thefe churches : For he being continued, by the
great goodnefs of God, in the profeffor's chair for
fo many years, moft by far of the minifters of this
and of fome neighbouring provinces, have been
trained up in their theological ftudies by and under
him ; who, I doubt not, do with one confent agree
to do him honour, as he who by his public and
private lectures, and perfonal conferences, has given
great light to them in the things of the gofpel;
and done a great deal to eftablifh them in many
important points of chriftianity. So in this way
his eminent gifts became of public ufe, and are as
it were, by their miniftry, tranfmitted to the feveral
churches of the land. And I believe his praife is
fo in thefe churches, efpecially with the minifters
of them, that they would with one voice declare
that they knew not any, who would have more, if
fo compleatly, filled that chair as he did.

IF we confider him in the government of the
college, and confulting for its welfare, he was a
very

family have, from time to time, for more than forty years
paft, been teftifying their pious and generous regards to
the college. And the prefent worthy Mr. Thomas Hollis,
of London, poffeffed abundantly of the fame excellent fpirit,
and kind regard to the college, which recommended and
endeared his great uncle to us, has fince the late deftruc-
tion of the library and apparatus by fire, fent towards the
reparation of that lofs, a very large collection of valuable
books, to the amount of fome hundreds fterling.
The Lord be praifed for that compaffionate, benevolent, and
liberal fpirit he has ftirred up towards the college of late ;
And may all its kind and generous benefactors, whether
in Great-Britain or amongft ourfelves, be abundantly re-
warded with the bleffings of divine providence and grace.

very ufeful member, not only confidered in his con-
nection with the prefident and tutors, in the imme-
diate government of the ftudents; but as one of the
corporation of the college. For, altho' his hardnefs
of hearing was a great difficulty to him when debates
were carried on, yet things being made known to
him (to have his thoughts upon them) there always
appeared in him fuch an accuracy of thought, fuch
a wifdom and judicioufnefs in his obfervations, as
were ever of great weight with us. Which I am
able to fpeak from my own obfervation, having had
the honour and pleafure of fitting with him at that
board for more than forty years.

AND fuch was the efteem the learned had of
his knowledge, fagacity, and foundnefs of judgment,
that he was much confulted in doubtful and difficult
cafes; and we never thought a controverfy in
better hands than when he was perfuaded to un-
dertake it. And altho' he was for defending and
fupporting the truth, and had an acutenefs, whereby
he could be keen in expofing the weaknefs of his
oppofers; yet chriftian candour and charity was
his fhining character; who went great lengths in his
charitable opinion of thofe who were fincere and
honeft in their differing fentiments from him.

IN his family relations he was very exemplary:
He was a tender and careful husband; a wife as
well as affectionate father; and a kind mafter. God
vifited him with fore afflictions in his family, in
many forrowful deaths, and in fore ficknefles and of
long continuance. But during fuch a feries of
troubles, God enabled him to exhibit a bright example

ample of patience and humble fubmiffion to the will
of God; and even fo much fedatenefs and com-
pofednefs of mind, that any one coming in to dif-
courfe with him upon any point, would hardly
perceive by him that there was any trouble in his
houfe. And he found it was good to hope, and
quietly wait for the falvation of God: For God
has been pleafed of late to fhift the fcene, and re-
ftore the voice of health and falvation, in a good
meafure, to his children; which I doubt not they
take notice of with thankfulnefs; and efpecially
that their tender father lived to fee them under fuch
comfortable circumftances before he left the world.

HE was a prudent, peaceable, friendly and kind
neighbour; ready to every good work of piety and
charity, as the poor and others can teftify : And we
all are witneffes, and God alfo, how holily, and
juftly, and unblameably, he behaved himfelf thro'
the whole courfe of his life among us.

AND now *mark the perfect man, and behold the
upright ; for the end of that man is peace.* His
death, like his life, was fedate and calm, without
any furprize or agitation of fpirit. He manifefted
to me, the day before he expired, " That if God
" had any further fervice for him to do he fhould
" be glad to live : But he was refigned to the will
" of God." And when I afked him, whether his
faith and hope remained ftrong and fteady? he
anfwered me to this purpofe, " He thought he
" could fay that in fome good meafure he had
" walked before God in truth and with a perfect
" heart : And altho' there had been many defects
" and

" and failings in his life, yet he hoped and believed
" that thro' Chrift he fhould be accepted." And
fo we all believe, and are perfuaded concerning him.

AND now what belongs to all of us, but to labour
to be duly affected with the death of an eminent
faint, and of fuch a diftinguifhed character ?

SURELY the college has great reafon to lament
the death of fuch a worthy, well accomplifhed and
faithful profeffor.

AND all the churches in the land have reafon to
lament the death of him whofe praife has been in
them. And may not only the ftudents who refide
at college, but all the minifters thro' the land, who
have been trained up under him, remember how
they have received and heard, and hold faft the
faithful and the good word they have received at
his mouth. And may we all unite in humble fer-
vent prayer, that the God of the fpirits of all flefh,
and with whom is the refidue of the fpirit, would
raife up and turn the eyes of the governors of the
college to a fucceffor in all refpects fitted for that
important ftation.

MAY the children of the deceafed be fupported
under fuch a bereaving difpenfation of divine providence ; and may a double portion of that good
fpirit which was in their father, and in their other
pious anceftors, defcend and reft upon them ; and
may they be very eminent bleffings in the feveral
ftations and fervices that God affigns to them ; and,
if it may be the will of God, as great bleffings to the
college as their excellent father has been.

MAY

MAY I myſelf, and this whole church and congregation, be deeply affected with the extinction of
this burning and ſhining light, whoſe devout pre-
ſence has for ſo many years graced this aſſembly;
and by whoſe kind labours, inſtructive, judicious and
accurate diſcourſes, we have been often entertained
and edified; to think we ſhall ſee his face and hear
his voice no more.

MAY thoſe of us who have for a long courſe of
years been concerned with the deceaſed in tranſact-
ing the various affairs of the college, deeply lay
to heart the great breach which by his death is
made upon the government of that ſociety: And
may God appear in great mercy to be. the ſpeedy
repairer of the breach.

FINALLY. May we all be quickened by this
holy providence to be up and doing; improving our
time, and our various talents, to the beſt advantage,
working the works of him who hath ſent us, whilſt
it is day; for the night of .death cometh, wherein
no man can work.

AND may thoſe of us who are much about the
age of our deceaſed friend and brother, be excited
to labour to be in actual readineſs for our own departure. Surely the voice of this providence is
the. voice of Chriſt to us in thoſe words, Luke xii.
35—37. with which I conclude. *Let your loins
be girded about, and your lights burning; and ye
yourſelves like unto men who wait for their Lord.
Bleſſed are thoſe ſervants whom the Lord when he
cometh ſhall find watching.* AMEN.

ORATIO FUNEBRIS,

IN OBITUM

EDVARDI WIGGLESWORTH, S.T.P.

QUAM,

IN SACELLO HOLDENIANO,

APUD COLLEGIUM HARVARDINUM,

INTER EFFERENDUM,

HABUIT

JOSEPHUS TAYLOR,

Collegii supra nominati alumnus.

" ----Confultiffimus vir---omnis DIVINI atque humani juris,---
quem juvenum æmulantium ftudia cœtus habuiffe conftat."
T. Livii, l. i. 18.

ORATIO FUNEBRIS.

ACTUM eft! vitam perfecit WIGGLES-
WORTH abfolvitque mortalem! Sic voluit
Pater omnipotens.---Fautores virtutis ac
humani generis amantes, vitâ defuncti, recordatione
uti fempiternâ vigeant, a viventibus repetere prope
fuo jure debent. Gratus quidem et animus monet,
inhumanum, quo tempore talium corpora terrâ con-
dantur, eodem et memoriam oblivione deleri. Hoc
fi debitum ulli poftulandum fuiffet, cui rectius quam
ei, cujus funebria jufta jam nunc facimus? At tem-
poris exiguitas, rigor hiemis, atque juventus mea,
quo minus omnes perpulchras. viri illius venerandi,
cujus reliquiæ fuper iftud trifte feretrum ponuntur,
virtutes etiam leviter attingam, aut mœftis cognatis
amicifque debitas adhibeam confolationes, vetant.

ALIIS

ALIIS liceat, aulæis retractis, mores in conspectu
ponere suavissimos, qui inde ab initio eum ad finem
usque vitæ præclarum reddidere. Penes alios sit
arbitrium illecebras depingendi eas, quæ intimo
sermoni erant decori ; eorumque, quibuscum ipsi
consuetudo erat, corda conciliârunt. Alii delincent
id virtutum sidus quod pectus illustravit : Horum in
munera non mihi est in animo irreptare; et hanc ob
causam plurima vitæ ornamenta silentio prætereo.

ECCE finis mortalium universorum! En viri
exitus honestissimi integerrimique, redimitus olivâ!
Aspicite reliquias viri, non solum de academiâ, sed
de republicâ etiam optime meriti! quem vivum
omnes boni in summo habebant honore; quem
mortuum summo mœrore lugent.

QUIS exuvias istius, jam quidem numero cælitum
adscripti, conspicere potest, qui non simul in memoriam revocet, quæ facultates insignes, quæ nobi-
lissimæ virtutes per totam vitam effulserint? Iis,
quæ sane doctum efficiunt, aliis fere omnibus longe
præstitit. In illo acerrimum ingenium, mens saga-
cissima, tenax memoria, rerum rectissime æstiman-
darum potestas eximie claruerunt. Omni ex parte
eruditus erat. Veterum peritus linguarum. In
historiâ tam civili quam ecclesiasticâ versatissimus.
Omnes denique, quibus vel minima cum professione
suâ intercessit cognatio, scientias penitus calluit.

Vi

Vi autem et acumine difceptandi præ cæteris eni-
tuit. Hac præfertim in re, fummo orbis literati
confenfu, tenuit primas, mirumque in modum re-
luxit. Hac vero facultate cùm plurimum valeret,
tum minime dogmaticus; neque, quas propofitiones
in medium protulerit, iis unquam, nifi gravibus
argumentis certifque fultis, affentiri voluit.

Cum primum equidem pietate infignis atque vir
honeftiffimus ille Dominus Hollis, jampridem
inter cælites relatus, Theologiæ Profeffionem, ab-
hinc quadraginta amplius annis, hoc loco inftituiffet,
ifte doctiffimus Profeffor, utpote etiam tum infigniter
idoneus, qui tali munere fungeretur, fuit electus.
Natura, quæ eum deftinaverat ad opus in quo
laboravit et excelluit, omnibus neceffariis, ut confilii
compos fieret, dotibus ornavit.

Theologiam vero profeffus eft; rebus ideo
divinis maxime ftuduit: Hîc erat percupidus emi-
nendi; hîc eminuit. Mente igitur præjudiciis ac
fuperftitione, humanitati fæpe fœdâ, fæpius fœdâ
religioni, exutâ, cùm omnia fedulo meditatus accu-
rateque fcrutatus effet, fententiarum de facris in
biblia, quæ fola ad homines in rebus tanti momenti
dirigendos data, fundamenta jecit. Confirmatis
demum fententiis, animum tantis doctrinæ copiis in-
ftruere, et ejufmodi corroborare argumentis, quibus
vires ad veritatem evangelii, adverfus malevolorum
impetus, confervandam, fuppeterent, erat curæ.

Conciones,

Conciones, tum pro roſtris publice pronun-
ciatæ, tum literis mandatæ et in lucem emiſſæ, ſtylo
materiæ ſemper conſonante; argumentis omnibus
ornamentis, quæ vel animum ſeducere, vel pravam
propenſionem voluntati ſolent injicere, nudatis, etſi
brevibus, nihilo tamen ſecius perſpicuis, quamvis
elaboratis, haud eo minus ſimplicibus, abſque meta-
phoris longe petitis, nervoſis; ordine nunquam non
naturali nec lucido, perpetuo documentis abundante;
diviſionibus paucis, at ſemper idoneis, a ſe invicem
ducentibus originem, et ad ipſam concluſionem,
creſcente vi, pergentibus; ad maximis utilitatibus
ſerviendum miris modis accommodatæ ſunt. Ut
verbo expediam—Cogitavit libere, nec de rebus
divinis dubitavit; diſputator, neque infidus; religioni
deditus, ſimul et a ſuperſtitione abhorrens.

ILLUM, profeſſoris officium præſtantem, inſpec-
temus; et quod tandem majus hoc fidelitatis exemplum ante oculos proponere queamus? Hoc facel-
lum, cujus ſacros intra parietes modò convenimus,
obteſtor, quanto cum labore hujus ſocietatis alumnos
ad Dei cultum erudiret, ac amore virtutis accenderet;
quam anxie ſe ad juveniles animos contra præjudicia
armandos pararet; neu ſententias a ſacris literis
alienas admitterent, propugnaret.

&c

HUNC ſi in privatâ verſatum vitâ luſtremus, in-
genü virum amabilis; animi benevolentis ac large
benefici; affabilitatis jucundiſſimæ; integrum vitæ,
                                                    ſine

fine labe fcelerifque purum; moribus ornatum fanc-
tiffimis; geftu gravem et venerabilem, apertum
tamen ac ingenuum; omnium denique imitatione
digniffimum; ab omnibus, ni virtutem perofis, di-
lectum effe, inveniemus.   Quæ virtutes quidem in
aliis afperæ atque feveræ videantur, in illo fane ve-
nufto renidebant decore.   Peramans conjugum.
Parens benevolentiffimus et benigniffimus.   Amicus
hofpitalis, munificus, conftans erat.   Omnes inter
viciffitudines vitæ, et cafus qui fibi domuique fuæ
divinitus contigerunt, fatis licèt in prefentiâ triftes,
tranquillus, continens, idem.

QUANTUM incommodi refpublica, quantum res
literaria, et hæc præcipue focietas; quantum amici
atque familiares, hujus ex morte, fuftinuerunt! Ubi
fama percrebuit, ibi capitur detrimentum; ubicun-
que autem terrarum literati habitant, eo equidem
emanaverat fama.

O WIGGLESWORTH! doctorum deliciæ, decus
doctrinæ, pietatis exemplum! ô WIGGLESWORTH
——vixifti!

The following Portrait of the DOCTOR's Character was drawn by one of his learned and much efteemed Friends, and inferted in the *Bofton Evening-Poft*, No. 1533.

Cambridge, January 19. 1765.

LAST Wednefday died here, in the 73d year of his age, after an illnefs of five days, the reverend and learned EDWARD WIGGLESWORTH, D. D. one of the Fellows of the Corporation, and HOLLIS Profeffor of Divinity in Harvard College : A Gentleman highly efteemed thro' life, and greatly lamented at his Death.

WE pretend not to draw a complete portrait of this eminent perfon, of whom it is not eafy to fay, whether he were more diftinguifhed by the vigor of his intellectual powers, by the extent of his knowledge, or the height of his moral attainments : We attempt only to fketch out fome of the principal lines of his character.

HE was fon of the late Rev. *Michael Wigglefworth* of *Malden*, who is well known throughout this country by his divine poems. He received his education in Harvard College, where he took his degree of Batchelor in Arts, in the year 1710, and proceeded Mafter in 1713, applying himfelf to the ftudy of divinity. He preached for fome time in different parifhes. When the late pious and generous THOMAS HOLLIS, Efq; of London founded a Profefforfhip of Divinity in this place, the governors of the College immediately turned their eyes upon Mr. WIGGLESWORTH, who was chofen the firft HOLLIS Profeffor of Divinity, June 28. 1721. and having been approved by the Founder, was publicly inftalled in that office in the College-Hall, October 24. 1722.

G   and

and was not long after chosen into the Corporation. He
continued to discharge the duties of his important office with
fidelity till within a few days of his death. Much the
greater part of the Ministers now living in this and the
neighbouring province, were formed under his instructions.
With what perspicuity and solidity he explained and
established the grand doctrines ●religion, with how critical
an accuracy, with how strict impartiality and amiable candor
he discussed the various points of controversy which have
so unhappily divided the christian world, all who have had
the advantage of his elaborate lectures, for more than forty
years past, can bear witness. Some of these discourses have
been made public for the benefit of others. They raised a
great esteem of their author. His character was still highten-
ed by some controversial pieces, which he published as
occasions required. Here he displayed in a nervous and
sufficiently animated style, yet in a cool and dispassionate
manner, such clearness and strength of argument, as left no
room for reply.

Being by an uncommon degree of deafness in a great
measure cut off from the pleasures of social converse, he had
more leisure to turn his attention inward;---to strengthen
the faculties of his mind and ripen his reflexions by habitual
meditation. This defect, as it deprived his friends of much
of the benefit of his conversation, so it debarred him
from some opportunities of more extensive usefulness. He
was for some time commissioner of the London society for
propagating the gospel among the Indians, but resigned
about ten years ago on account of his increasing deafness.
He was chosen one of the Scotch deputation for propagating
christian knowledge, about four years since, but excused himself on the same account. For this reason he declined the
Rectorship of Yale-College, New-Haven, when it was offered
him. The Univerfity of Edinburg gave their strongest
testimonial of his merit, by sending him● Diploma for a
Doctorate in Divinity. It bears date June 2. 1730.

IN his private life, the Gentleman and the Chriſtian appeared to great advantage. He was of an affable, con-deſcending and obliging diſpoſition. Gentle to all, he was in the higheſt degree tender to his conſorts deceaſed, and his children, under the maladies of many years continuance, with which it pleaſed GOD to viſit them. During this ſeaſon of long diſtreſs, aggravated too by very preſſing diffi-culties ariſing from the narrowneſs of his circumſtances, he preſerved an unruffled calmneſs, a moſt exemplary patience and ſubmiſſion to the will of Heaven. Not a repining word was heard from his lips. He had a heart that felt deeply for the unhappineſs of others; and he conſtantly appropri-ated a tenth part of his income, contracted as it was, to pious and charitable uſes. On every account he was ſolici-tous to maintain the honor of the chriſtian character. The ſame equable firmneſs and compoſure of mind, which had attended him thro' life, held to the laſt; and the ſerenity with which he met the approach of death, as it was ſup-ported by the enlivening hope of an happy immortality, afforded a ſtriking inſtance of the divine power and excellency of the chriſtian religion. " Mark the perfect man, and " behold the upright; for the end of that man is peace." Pſa. xxxvii. 37.

HE was interred this afternoon with great reſpect, the Miniſters and many other Gentlemen from the neighbouring towns attending his funeral, which agreeably to his own deſire, was conducted in the method lately introduced. His corpſe, preceded by the ſcholars, was carried into the HOLDEN Chapel, where a funeral oration was pronounced by one of the ſenior Students.

HIS only ſon is now a Tutor in the College; and his only ſurviving daughter married to Mr. Sewall, lately choſen HANCOCK Profeſſor of Hebrew and other oriental languages.

The poetical Effay fubjoined was wrote by a young gentleman, a ftudent in the College, and publifhed in the Maffachufets Gazette, No. 3179.

Sacred to the Memory of Dr. WIGGLESWORTH.

THE prophet's foul has bid adieu to earth,
 Soar'd on cœleftial wings, and gain'd its home;
 It's native home, where kindred fpirits throng,
 To bid it welcome to the heavenly fhores.
Forgive my mufe, if in the general grief,
Which paints a folemn gloom in ev'ry face,
She drops a tear o'er his black-mantled urn,
And mourns his exit from a weeping world.

 T' eradicate the paffions from the foul,
To be unmov'd with depths of human woe,
Whate'er the Stoicks fay, is all a dream :
Who knew our frame, of man the greateft friend,
JESUS, by his own tears at *Laz'rus'* tomb
Mark'd the juft debt to our departed friends.
Roufe, roufe, my mufe, in numbers celebrate
The fage divine and venerable faint :
Who, firm and placid, ran the earthly race,
His heart unmov'd, his life without a ftain.

 Strong and capacious were his mental pow'rs ;
His judgment clear and found ; his diction pure ;
His ev'ry word and line, full fraught with fenfe,
Deep thought befpoke and treafures all his own.
Great were his talents in defence of truth :
'Twas here he fhone with a diftinguifh'd ray.

How

How would he ftrip fophiftic arguments
Of ev'ry fpecious glare, that leads aftray
From truth's unerring paths, th' unwary mind!
How, with his cogent reafons, ftrongly urge
The grand, th' important doctrines of his Lord;
'Till, clear'd of all obfcurity and doubt,
His fubjects fhone bright as the noon-day fun!

Ye fons of Harvard, fay; for ye can tell,
Who once, fo highly bleft, fat at his feet
And catch'd th' inftructive accents from his tongue,
His weighty truft how faithfully difcharg'd;
How fteady he purfu'd that noble aim —
To form your morals, to infpire your hearts
With love of virtue, and pure wifdom's ways;
To fill your minds with all-important truths.
Oh WIGGLESWORTH! could wifdom, learning, fenfe,
Protect their fons, and fave them from the tomb:
Could meeknefs, charity, and ev'ry grace,
That e'er combin'd t' adorn a human foul,
Their vot'ries fnatch from death's rapacious jaws,
Sure thou, bleft fhade, hadft ne'er become his prey.

Ye indigent, bewail the generous man,
Whofe heart humane has felt for your diftrefs;
Whofe lib'ral hand has oft fupply'd your wants,
And dealt it's Godlike favours all around.
He is no more! no more fhall ye partake
Thofe kind reliefs he bounteoufly beftow'd.

Ye children of the dear departed faint,
Witnefs your parent's love, whofe tender breaft
Felt all your joys, partook of all your griefs.
Wife were his counfels, gentle his reproofs:
In ev'ry act parental love appear'd:
His conduct tended to excite efteem,
And filial piety within the breaft.

But

But now, alas ! of such a tender fire
Bereft, what words can speak the depths of woe !
The matchless Grecian painter, when he drew
The horrors in each countenance, express'd
At sight of *Iphigenia* sacrific'd,
Near Aulis, on the cruel Grecian shores,
Despairing of his skill to represent
Her agonizing father's deep distress,
Conceal'd his face beneath his mantling robe.
And wisely left the world to guess that grief,
That anguish which his pencil could not paint.
Thus cease, my pen, t' attempt th' unequal task,
To picture woe which silence better speaks
Than all th' expressive language mortals use.

　Ye friends of virtue, friends of the deceas'd,
Come mingle tears, and vent your gen'rous sighs ;
Weep o'er the man, whose tongue was wont to charm
Your captivated hearts ; while in discourse
From his warm breast, by social virtues fir'd,
You catch'd an equal flame.-------------
True, was his friendship, for his open heart
Nor knew deceit, nor brook'd the least disguise.
Serene his temper undisturb'd by cares ;
His mind sedate in ev'ry scene of life,
Display'd the christian, who unmov'd by ills,
Can sit and smile, while earth's foundations shake.

　While some, whose lives for virtue were renown'd,
Who pass'd for christians of distinguish'd rank,
Cou'd only boast of some few shining deeds,
Like scatter'd stars o'er Æther's vast expanse ;
His ev'ry year, with virtuous actions crown'd,
Glow'd like the milky way, thick set with stars.
Witness, ye walls, where contemplation reign'd ;
Where he his thoughtful hours, unweary'd, spent,
Witness the fervour of his heav'nly mind ;

How

[4,]

How, while he mus'd on themes divinely bright,
His raptur'd foul to empyrean flies.
Has wing'd it's way, and view'd the bleft abodes,
Where joys perennial dwell, whence blifsful ftreams
Of pleafures, ever new, flow without end ;
And ravifh'd faints forever tune their voice,
To fing that love which rais'd them to thofe feats.
Then has he wifh'd to quit his earthly frame,
Which kept his foul a pris'ner here confin'd,
And long'd to join th' affembled choirs above,
To prove thofe joys, and mix his fongs with their's.

Let this our forrows foothe, and dry our tears,
That death, the laft of foes, has loft his fting.
Has prov'd a friend to loofe the weary foul,
And raife it to the realms of endlefs blifs.
Now he imbibes full draughts of heav'nly joy,
From living fprings faft by the throne of God ;
His foul is free to range the azure fields,.
And fweets inhale from ev'ry fragrant flow'r.
Ceafe then, ye tears, and ceafe, each murm'ring figh;
Be ev'ry paffion hufh'd.—He reigns with Chrift.

Ye, who furvive, thofe virtues make your own,
Which fhone confpicuous thro' his holy life :
This will embalm his precious mem'ry more
Than panegyrics of fublimeft ftrain.

SYMPATHES.

www.ingramcontent.com/pod-product-compliance
Lightning Source LLC
Chambersburg PA
CBHW021638270326
41931CB00008B/1075